Pebble® Plus

AMAZING SIGHTS OF THE SKY

Northern Lights

by Martha E. H. Rustad

CAPSTONE PRESS
a capstone imprint

Pebble Plus is published by Capstone Press,
1710 Roe Crest Drive, North Mankato, Minnesota 56003
www.mycapstone.com

Library of Congress Cataloging-in-Publication Data
Library of Congress Cataloging-in-Publication data is available on the Library of Congress website.

ISBN 978-1-5157-6751-0 (library binding)
ISBN 978-1-5157-6757-2 (paperback)
ISBN 978-1-5157-6769-5 (eBook PDF)

Summary: Simple text introduces readers to the Northern Lights, or aurora borealis, including
why they occur, where they can be seen, and how often they color the sky.

Editorial Credits
Anna Butzer, editor; Juliette Peters, designer; Wanda Winch, media researcher;
Steve Walker, production specialist

Photo Credits
Alamy Stock Photo: blickwinkel/Baesemann, 19; Getty Images Inc: Paul Hardy - Concept Stills
and Motion, 21; iStockphoto: Justinreznick, 17; Shutterstock: Alesandro14, blue and green aurora
background, Frozenmost, cover, Jurik Peter, 11, Kati Molin, 15, Mohd Zaki Shamsudin, 9, muratart,
13, Pigprox, 1, Shin Okamoto, 5; Thinkstock: iStockphoto/surangaw, 7

Note to Parents and Teachers

The Amazing Sights of the Sky set supports national science standards related to earth science. This
book describes and illustrates Northern Lights. The images support early readers in understanding
the text. The repetition of words and phrases helps early readers learn new words. This book also
introduces early readers to subject-specific vocabulary words, which are defined in the Glossary
section. Early readers may need assistance to read some words and to use the Table of Contents,
Glossary, Read More, Internet Sites, Critical Thinking Questions, and Index sections of the book.

Printed and bound in the United States of America.
112017   010943R

Table of Contents

What Are Northern Lights?

Green and purple
waves dance across
the night sky.
The Northern Lights
look beautiful tonight.

The Northern Lights are an aurora. Their full name is the aurora borealis. These colorful lights are often seen near the North Pole.

There are lights near the South Pole too. They are called the Southern Lights, or aurora australis. These lights can be seen in South America and Australia.

Why Do Auroras Shine?

Storms on the sun lead to auroras on Earth. Solar winds travel through space. The winds carry tiny bits of energy from the sun.

The North and South Poles act like magnets. They draw solar winds toward them. Solar energy crashes into gases near Earth. These crashes make colorful auroras.

sun

Earth

Green, red, blue, and purple lights flash during auroras.

Different gases make different colors.

Auroras seem to move like clouds.

See the Northern Lights

Auroras happen all the time.

But we can see them only at night.

Winter nights are long and dark.

People see auroras more often during winter.

Scientists keep track of storms on the sun. Check the aurora forecast to find a good night for Northern Lights.

Dress warmly.

Go away from city lights.

Let your eyes get used to the dark.

You will see an amazing sight!

21

GLOSSARY

aurora—lights given off when solar bits crash into gases near the Earth

forecast—a prediction for when something will happen

gas—a substance that expands and flows freely

magnet—a metal that attracts metal; the North and South Poles act like magnets

Northern Lights—aurora near the North Pole; they are also called aurora borealis

Southern Lights—aurora near the South Pole; they are also called aurora australis

sun—the large star at the center of our solar system

READ MORE

Hunter, Nick. *Northern Lights.* The Night Sky: And Other Amazing Sights in Space. Chicago: Capstone Heinemann Library, 2013.

Peters, Elisa. *Auroras: Behind the Northern and Southern Lights.* Nature's Mysteries. New York: Rosen Educational Services, 2017.

Rajczak, Kristen. *The Northern Lights.* Nature's Light Show. New York: Gareth Stevens Pub., 2013.

INTERNET SITES

Use FactHound to find Internet sites related to this book.

Visit *www.facthound.com*

Just type in 9781515767510 and go.

 Check out projects, games and lots more at
www.capstonekids.com

CRITICAL THINKING QUESTIONS

1. Where do you need to be to see the Southern Lights?

2. In what season can you see more auroras?

3. What does solar energy crash into to make auroras?

INDEX